The True Story of "America's First Daughter," Martha 'Patsy' Jefferson

Geraldine Brooks
(born 1875)

Reprinted from:
Dames and Daughters of the Young Republic
By Geraldine Brooks
T. Y. Crowell & Company, 1901

D1528848

MARTHA JEFFERSON, DAUGHTER OF THOMAS JEFFERSON.

Born at Monticello, Sept. 27, 1773. Died at Edgehill, Oct. 10, 1836.

"As a child she was her father's only comforter in the great sorrow of his life, in maturer years she was his intimate friend and companion; her presence lent to his home its greatest charm and her love and sympathy were his greatest solace in the troubles that clouded the evening of his life."—Miss S. Randolph.

IN the autumn of the year 1784 a little American girl found herself in the midst of French convent life at the Abbage Royale de Panthemont. She was a very unhappy little girl. Not even the pretty red frock which she wore, with its red cuffs and tucker, the uniform of the convent school, could comfort her. When her schoolmates were chatting merrily together in a language of which she did not understand a word, she looked sadly on or stole away to sit by herself thinking of her beautiful home on the "little mountain," of the flowers that grew there, of the walks through the woods, and the wild horseback rides over the hills, of her vanished freedom, and most of all of her indulgent papa, to whom she had been wont to say her lessons and from whom, no matter how stupid or naughty she had been, she had received only words of encouragement and love.

The nuns watched the little American girl and the scholars watched her. They were very sorry for her. Never before, it seemed to them, had they beheld so homesick a little mortal. They saw her turn away from them and weep bitterly many times a day. But in the evening they noticed a great change. Then her tears were wiped away and she sat by the convent window eager and expectant.

The reason for her transformation was known to all. She was waiting for a gentleman, a very tall gentleman, with sandy hair and kind blue eyes. He came to see the little American every evening, and when he arrived she was all smiles and sunshine.

The gentleman, too, was happy in the meeting. He kissed the little girl tenderly, asked if she had been a good girl that day, hoped that she was getting to love her school and her teachers and her fellow pupils, inquired playfully how many French words she had learned since he last saw her, asked if she was mastering the grammar and wanted to know how many hours she had devoted to sewing and how many to music. Then, as the two sat side by side, he stroked her hair and told her he was glad to see it so neatly combed, remarked with satisfaction on the tidiness of her appearance, straightened a bow here and a ruffle there, and declared that he wished he might never see her carelessly attired, for no one, he said, could ever love a slovenly little girl. One would have thought to hear him talk that he was mother as well as father to the child.

The little girl, Patsy, he lovingly called her, listened attentively to all that he had to say. She answered his inquiries as bravely as she could. But when it came her turn to question and remark, her talk was not of the convent but of home. She wanted to know what he supposed Aunt Eppes was doing and little sister Polly; she wondered if the bluebirds and robins were still singing in her favorite willow tree and the redbud and the dogwood blossoming in the meadow. She remarked that she thought this would have been a fine day for a mountain climb or a frolic on horseback over the fields, and she asked wistfully if he did wish that they might go away from France, back to dear, beautiful Monticello, never to leave it again.

Poor Patsy I Even as she spoke she knew that it would be a long while before she could behold once more her "dear, beautiful Monticello." She was learning the hard lesson which other dames and daughters of our earliest statesmen learned, that a man sacrifices his home and family when he devotes himself to the service of his country. Of course she rejoiced in her father's greatness. She delighted to speak of him as "Plenipotentiary to Europe," and she always announced with very evident pride the fact that she was the daughter of Thomas Jefferson. But nevertheless she could not help her longings for a lost happiness, a happiness that was nowhere else but on top of the little mountain, in the society of those who had their dwelling there.

When Patsy thought of the little mountain, as she did many times a day, she did not only recall it as the home from which she had just departed. Her memory went back to the days of her earliest childhood, when another than her father had been the guiding spirit of Monticello. She remembered her mother, a beautiful, gentle-mannered woman, as firm as she was sweet and gracious. Her word, Patsy recollected, spoken in low, soft tones, was law in the Jefferson home, and she, not the father, had reproved and disciplined the children for their faults and blunders.

Her father's devotion to her mother was among Patsy's most vivid memories. Mrs. Jefferson had always been delicate and Mr. Jefferson, Patsy could remember, was ever mindful of her health, shielding her from drafts, seeing that she always had a comfortable chair and a hassock under her feet, following her into the garden with shawl and sunshade and stealing time from his affairs of state, whenever such a theft was possible, to walk and ride with her through the beautiful country that surrounded their Virginia home.

The period of her mother's death and of her father's grief was a time which Patsy dared not recall, even to herself. She was then only ten years old, of an age when she most needed mother love and mother care, but her own sorrow was almost forgotten in the contemplation of that greater sorrow which was before her. We are given a glimpse into the lonely desolate house where, in the solitude of his own chamber, for three weeks, a man "walked incessantly night and day, only lying down occasionally when nature was completely exhausted." The full extent of his grief was known to none, not even to the kind, devoted sisters who stayed with him and watched over him most tenderly. But Patsy understood when, one night, she entered her father's room almost by stealth and found him giving way to a paroxysm of weeping. And in the days that followed, when finally he left his room and rode about the mountain on horseback over the least frequented paths, she was his constant companion, his one comforter in this, the greatest sorrow of his life.

Memories of the months that followed that saddest period in Patsy's young life were still fresh in her mind. She recalled very vividly the time that she and her sisters, pretty little Polly and the baby Lucy, had left Monticello and gone to the home of one of their father's friends in Chesterfield County, there to be inoculated for the smallpox. Their father had been their nurse upon that trying occasion, and Patsy could well remember his gentleness and tenderness with them. She felt that no other father than hers could so well have filled a mother's place.

It was at that time, Patsy recollected, while she and her sisters were still undergoing the troubles of inoculation, that word came of her father's appointment as Plenipotentiary to Europe, to be associated with Dr. Franklin and Mr. Adams in negotiating peace. Of course Patsy was not old enough to comprehend all that her father's new position meant. She was principally occupied with the thought that he was going to France and that she was going with him. And as she looked back upon that time of preparation and departure she felt that she could never forget her pain at parting with her beloved Monticello and with her dear little sisters, who had to be left behind in the care of their Aunt and Uncle Eppes and in the congenial society of their cousins, the numerous little Eppeses.

Patsy remembered, too, very distinctly, the long, tedious journey to Philadelphia. To the shy little girl within the coach, sole companion of a gentleman, surrounded and gazed upon by strange faces, those hours of travel seemed almost interminable. Yet, whatever her trials and hardships, she was willing to endure them rather than give up the pleasure and happiness of being with her father. To be with him always and under all circumstances was the first wish of her heart.

To her stay in Philadelphia Patsy's thoughts reverted with considerable pleasure. She had made many friends there and enjoyed many good times. It was a surprise to her that she remained in the city as long as she did; but news received by Congress from Europe delayed her father's departure to the Old World, so, for a while, she and he made their home in Philadelphia. It was Patsy's introduction to city life. She was placed at a seminary for young girls under the care of Mrs. Hopkinson, "an excellent and kind lady," so tradition describes her. There Patsy had her first real schooling. Formerly her one instructor had been her father. Of course she thought none of her new instructors as wise as he, but she enjoyed her school and loved to talk to her father of the books she was reading and the tunes she was playing and of the progress she was making in dancing and drawing. She even confided to him her fears arising from the superstitions of the time, to which he replied with his usual sophistry: "I hope you will have good sense enough to disregard those foolish predictions that the world is to be at an end soon," he said. "The Almighty has never made known to anybody at what time he created it; nor will he tell anybody when he will put an end to it, if he ever means to do it."

At length the time arrived for Patsy to say good-by to her new school and her new friends and to all things American. She and her father embarked for Europe in the early summer of the year 1784. Patsy retained very pleasant memories of the voyage across. She thus, described it in a letter to one of her Philadelphia friends: "We had a lovely passage in a beautiful new ship, that had made but one passage before. There were only six passengers, all of whom Papa knew, and a fine sunshine all the way, with a sea which was as calm as a river."

The trip across the channel to France, it would seem, Patsy did not find nearly so enjoyable. "It rained violently all the way," she wrote, "and the sea was exceedingly rough. The *cabane* was not more than three feet wide and about four feet long. There was no other furniture than an old bench which was fast to the wall. The door by which we came in at was so little that one was obliged to enter on all fours. There were two little doors on the side of the *cabane*, the way to our beds, which was composed of two boxes and a couple of blankets, without either a bed or mattress, so that I was obliged to sleep in my clothes. There being no window in the *cabane* we were obliged to stay in the dark, for fear of the rain coming in if we opened the door." Poor Patsy! If such were her surroundings we do not wonder that she was glad to emerge from the darkness and stuffiness of the little *cabane* into the glad sunshine of a beautiful morning in France.

Yet even the pleasant French weather and the pretty French scenery could not make Patsy happy. The strangeness of everything, the foreign tongue, the foreign sights, the foreign customs quite dazed her. Her father, too, was a little confused by that first glimpse of France. "We would have fared badly," wrote Patsy, "if an Irish gentleman, an entire stranger to us, seeing our embarrassment, had not been so good as to conduct us to a house and was of great service to us."

Of the journey inland to Paris, Patsy declared, "We should have had a very delightful voyage to Paris, for Havre de Grace is built at the mouth of the Seine and we follow the river all the way through the most beautiful country I ever saw in my life,—it is a perfect garden,—if the singularity of our carriage (a phaeton) had not attracted the attention of all we met; and whenever we stopped we were surrounded by beggars—one day I counted no less than nine where we stopped to change horses."

Patsy laughed whenever she recalled the day of her arrival in Paris. She did not celebrate the completion of her long journey, after the manner of some of her Puritan neighbors at home, with fasting and prayer. But, being in Paris, the city of fashions and frivolities, and having arrived there a dusty and travel-worn little woman, all her time and attention was given to the grave matter of clothes. "We were obliged to send immediately," wrote Patsy, "for the stay-maker, the mantuamaker, the milliner, and even the shoemaker before I could go out. I never had the friseur but once, but I soon got rid of him and turned down my hair in spite of all they could say."

To Patsy's troubled mind all that seemed long ago now. Her days at the convent had pushed everything that had happened before away back in the distance. After her first week in the Abbage she felt that she had been spending half of her lifetime there.

But very soon time began to pass more quickly. Though Patsy was at first so shy and homesick, she was naturally a very happy little girl, full of fun and laughter. It was impossible for her to be mournful very long. She gradually became accustomed to the new surroundings. She began to speak French, at first hesitatingly and brokenly, but with more and more fluency as time went on. She also began to make friends and after a while she came to be known among her special chums, the English girls Julia and Bettie, and the French Mademoiselles de Botedoux and De Chateaubrun, as "Jeff" and "Jeffie."

We catch glimpses of Patsy and her convent life as they come to us from the pages of her own letters and the letters of her friends. The Abbage, it seems, was a very aristocratic institution, "the best and most genteel school in Paris," records John Adams' observant young daughter. The nuns who had it in charge "belonged," we are told, "to the best families in Europe and were born and bred ladies," while "the pupils were from the highest classes of society, being the daughters of the gentlemen and diplomatic men of various countries and of the nobility and gentry of France." There at the Abbage the "best instruction" was to be had and "the best masters for accomplishments" and the best sort of fun as well, which latter consideration in the minds of Miss Patsy and all the other pupils was as important as any other.

Indeed so highly aristocratic was the Abbage that no pupil was admitted there without the recommendation of a lady of rank. Patsy herself had entered on the good word of a "lady friend" of her father's friend the Marquis de la Fayette. The lady who spoke the good word became interested in Patsy. She had some curiosity to see how her shy little protegee might develop. One day she went to pay a visit at the Abbage, after Patsy had been living there about a year. She arrived when the girls were all at play in the garden and she sat down beside the window to watch them. Among the girls she noted especially a tall, aristocratic-looking girl. "Who is that?" she asked with interest, of the nun who sat beside her. The nun looked at the lady with some surprise. "Why, madame," she replied, "that is your protegee, Mademoiselle Jefferson." The lady smiled, and nodded her head in satisfaction. "Oh, indeed," she exclaimed, "she has a very distinguished air."

Thus we see that from the diffident little homesick maiden of a year before Patsy had developed into a person of consideration and importance. Her life at the convent had given all the needed confidence and self-reliance. During that year she had enjoyed, too, the broadening influence that came from occasional visits with her father and peeps into the Parisian world.

We find mention of these visits and peeps in the diary of Miss Adams, daughter of John Adams, who was in Paris at the same time that Patsy was. Miss Adams, though several years Patsy's senior, was very much attracted toward her little countrywoman and wrote of her, "Miss Jefferson is a sweet girl, delicacy and sensibility are read in every feature and her manners are in unison with all that is amiable and lovely," certainly high praise from a young woman of Miss Adams' aristocratic and fastidious taste.

The associate work of their fathers brought the two girls very often together, and we occasionally discover such entries as these in the entertaining pages of Miss Adams' diary. "When we had finished our business we went to Mr. Jefferson's where I saw Miss J., a most amiable girl;" and again, "To-day we dined with Mr. Jefferson. He invited us to come and see all Paris which is to be seen in the streets to-day, and many masks, it being the last day but one of the

Carnival. Miss Jefferson dined with us; no other company."

It is in Miss Adams' diary, too, that we read an announcement of the death of Patsy's sister Lucy, the baby who, with little Polly, had been left behind in America in the care of Aunt and Uncle Eppes and all the little Eppeses. Under the date of Jan. 27, 1785, Miss Adams records, "A small company to dine to-day. Miss Jefferson we expected, but the news of the death of one of Mr. J.'s children in America, brought by the Marquis de la Fayette, prevented. Mr. J. is a man of great sensibility and parental affection. His wife died when the child was born, and he was almost in a confirmed state of melancholy, confined himself from the world and even from his friends for a long time; and this news has greatly affected him and his daughter."

The death of this baby was indeed an affliction to Patsy and her father. Mr. Jefferson became anxious about the other little daughter whom he had left behind him. He referred to her as "my dear little Polly who hangs on my thoughts night and day." He wrote to Mrs. Eppes to send her to him. But Polly preferred America to France. She sent a letter to her papa saying that she did not "want to go," that she had "rather stay " with Aunt Eppes and Cousin Jacky.

Her unwillingness only made her father all the more eager for her coining. He did not like to think that she was learning to forget her papa and her sister Patsy, and that others were taking their places in her heart. He insisted that "the little lady" as he called her, in spite of her hopes and prayers to remain in Virginia, should be despatched to France.

So Polly was despatched. But it was only by means of a trick that she was gotten from her native land. For several days she and her playfellow cousins had been taken for a frolic on board a ship that was lying at anchor in the harbor. Finally one afternoon Polly grew drowsy and fell asleep. When she awoke her friends were gone, the shore was out of sight, and she and her maid were tossing in the midst of a scene that was all blue sky and blue ocean, conscious that each roll was carrying them further and further away from Cousin Jacky and Aunt Eppes and home. Poor little Polly! Her heart was almost broken.

Polly made her voyage to Europe in the summer of 1787. She landed in England and was met there by the Adamses, who had moved from Paris to London. Mrs. Adams took charge of the beautiful frightened child, and Polly and the future Mistress President became great friends. Mrs. Adams has left in her letters a charming picture of Miss Polly: "I have had with me," she wrote, "a little daughter of Mr. Jefferson's, who arrived here with a young negro girl, her servant, from Virginia.

Mr. Jefferson wrote me some months ago that he expected them and desired me to receive them. I did so, and was amply repaid for my trouble. A finer child of her age I never saw. She is not eight years old. She would sit sometimes and describe to me the parting with her aunt, and the love she had for her little cousins, till the tears would stream down her cheeks; and how I had been her friend and she loved me. She clung round me so that I could not help shedding a tear at parting with her. She was the favorite of every one in the house."

At length the time came for Polly to join her father and Patsy in France. "A trusty servant," so Mr. Jefferson tells us, was sent to London to bring their little traveller to them. There is something quite pathetic in Mr. Jefferson's story of her meeting with them. So long a while had she been parted from them that when she first saw them, as Mr. Jefferson declared, "she neither knew us nor should we have known her had we met with her unexpectedly."

Her father's and her sister's love, however, soon won little Polly's heart and made her feel at home with them. Patsy would not allow her to be lonely and left the convent for a time to devote herself to her. Mr. Jefferson tells of how Patsy "came and staid a week with Polly leading her from time to time to the convent until she became familiarized to it." And he adds, "She (Polly) is now established in the convent perfectly happy, a universal favorite with all the young ladies and the mistresses."

Of Patsy herself, in the same letter, which was written to Mrs. Eppes, Mr. Jefferson remarks "Patsy enjoys good health. She has grown much the last year or two and will be very tall. She retains all her anxiety to get back to her country and her friends, particularly yourself. Her dispositions give me perfect satisfaction and her progress is well."

The letters that passed between Patsy and her father at this period are very interesting. They show what a happy comradeship existed between the two. She talks to him of her school life and lessons: he advises and comforts her in all her schoolgirl difficulties. And throughout their correspondence there breathes always an affection that was to both of them the chief blessing of life.

"Nobody in this world," he tells her, "can make me so happy or so miserable as you. To your sister and yourself I look to render the evening of my life serene and contented. Its morning has been clouded by loss after loss till I have nothing left but you. My expectations of you are high, yet not higher than you may attain. I do not doubt either your affections or your dispositions. Industry and resolution only are wanting. Be industrious, then, my dear child. Think nothing unsurmountable by resolution and application and you will be all that I wish you to be."

And Patsy answers with a determination that shows how eager she was to be all that her father "wished her to be." "You say your expectations of me are high," she writes, "yet not higher than I can attain. Then be assured, my dear papa, that you shall be satisfied in that, as well as in anything else that lies in my power; for what I hold most precious is your satisfaction, indeed I should be miserable without it."

With this thought always in mind, that she must fulfil her father's hopes of her, Patsy gave her attention to her studies. She reported her progress in them to her father with a frankness and artlessness that proved her to be a child as well as an ambitious little woman. "I have begun a beautiful tune with Baltastre," she wrote, "done a very pretty landscape with Pariseau—a little man playing on a violin—and begun another beautiful landscape."

Her Latin seems to have been her one stumblingblock. "I go on slowly with my Tite Live (Livy)," she confessed; "it being in such ancient Italian that I cannot read without my master and very little with him even;" and again, still struggling with her Livy, she wrote, "Titus Livius puts me out of my wits. I cannot read a word by myself, and I read of it very seldom with my master."

Her father could not endure to have her fail in the accomplishment of anything. He besought her to get the better of her Latin and argued with her in his usual logical and persuasive fashion. "I do not like your saying that you are unable to read the ancient print of your Livy but with the aid of your master," he declared. "We are always equal to what we undertake with resolution. It is a part of the American character to surmount every difficulty by resolution and contrivance. In Europe there are shops for every want; its inhabitants, therefore, have no idea that their wants can be supplied otherwise. Remote from all other aid *we* are obliged to invent and to execute; to find means within ourselves and not to lean on others. Consider, therefore, the conquering of your Livy as an exercise in the habit of surmounting difficulties, a habit which will be very necessary to you in the country where you are to live."

It was in this way, never hesitating to give the why and wherefore of a case when it was needed, that Jefferson directed his daughter in the pursuits and the conduct of her life. "The object most interesting to me for the residue of my life," he told her, "will be to see you developing daily those principles of virtue and goodness which will make you valuable to others and happy in yourself, and acquiring those talents and that degree of science which will guard you at all times against *ennui*, the most dangerous poison of life. A mind always employed is always happy. This is the true secret, the grand receipt for felicity. Be good and industrious and you will be what I most love in the world."

Such words as these, not disagreeable "preachy" words, but wise, kind, fatherly words, are constantly appearing in Jefferson's letters to his daughter, and as we read them we do not wonder that Patsy considered them the chief incentive to success amid the trials and difficulties of schoolgirl life. They used always to fill her with fresh courage and determination. "I am not so industrious as you or I would wish," she would answer, "but I hope that in taking pains I very soon shall be. I have already begun to study more. I am learning a very pretty thing now (on the harpsichord). I have drawn several little flowers all alone that the master even has not seen. I shall take up my Livy, as you desire it. I shall begin it again as I have lost the thread of the history."

Yet, in spite of good intentions and brave efforts, Patsy did not conquer all things. She was too human not to fail occasionally. Though she won an easy victory over all her other studies, Livy remained a most invincible adversary. "I have learnt several new pieces on the harpsichord," she wrote, "drawn five landscapes and three flowers, and hope to have done something more by the time you come. I go on pretty well with my history. But as for Tite Live I have begun it three or four times and go on so slowly with it that I believe I never shall finish it. It was in vain that I took courage; it serves to little good in a thing almost impossible. I read a little of it with my master who tells me almost all the words and, in fine, it makes me lose my time."

The period was drawing near when Livy, and with him all the other study books, were to be discarded and laid upon the shelf. Patsy's last year at the convent arrived. She became an important, privileged person. She dined at the Abbess' table, she helped to entertain the guests of the convent, and she received instruction in all the fine points of etiquette which she would need when, a year later, a well informed and accomplished debutante, she was to enter the gay society of Paris.

Yet even while Patsy was being prepared for the momentous step that was to carry her out of the quiet shadows of the convent into the brilliant light of the Parisian world, she was dreaming of a life very different from that which her father and friends were planning for her. She was a young girl, warm-hearted, impulsive, and impressionable. She loved the nuns who had been her guardians and friends for so many years and she thought that she would like to be as one of them, living always in an atmosphere of pure thoughts and self-sacrificing deeds. During her leisure moments she was often to be seen walking and talking with the nuns and with the Abbe Edgeworth de Fermont, he who at a later day was to accompany the unfortunate Louis the Sixteenth, as his last confessor, to the guillotine. The Catholic religion as interpreted by these good people seemed to the young Protestant better and truer than her own, and one day, with the spirit of their words upon her, she wrote to her father, from whom she had no secret, telling the story of her change of faith and expressing the wish that she might be a nun.

Mr. Jefferson did not answer Patsy by letter. He acted upon the occasion with his usual sensibleness and tact. After waiting a day or two he drove to the convent, had a private interview with the Abbess, and then asked to see his daughters. When Patsy and Polly came into the room he greeted them with more than the usual warmth of affection, and told them that he had come to take them away from school. He was tired of living alone, he said, and he wanted his daughters at home with him.

So Patsy and Polly said good-by to the convent and drove away with their father. It is needless to state that Patsy did not refer to her letter. She had read her father's answer to it in his face. At his request she let herself be carried into the gay whirl of Parisian society, and her new religious convictions and her dreams of a rosary and a solitary cell were soon forgotten in the healthy girlish enjoyment of finery, balls, and beaux.

Patsy was sixteen when she entered the world of Paris, and was introduced into the brilliant court

of Louis the Sixteenth. In spite of her youth and her modest, retiring disposition, she was considered a remarkable young woman. She did credit to the excellent education which she had received. She was found to be a good linguist, an accomplished musician, and one well versed in matters literary and historical. She was not beautiful (and perhaps it is a relief to posterity to learn that she was not,

24

after hearing of so many dames and daughters of a bygone day whose wondrous fairness is forever being told in story and rehearsed in song). She is reputed to have been "tall and stately," and to have had an interesting rather than a pretty face. It was not so much for harmony of form and feature, but it was for the charm of her conversation and manner, for the amiability of her disposition, and for the sweet unselfishness of her character that she was universally admired.

Hints of Miss Patsy's good times and of the interesting people with whom she met, when she was a debutante in the Paris world, have come down to us. We read of her pleasant acquaintance with the English ladies of Tufton, who sometimes acted as her chaperones, and with the duke of Dorset and his nieces; of her friendship with the gay and gallant Marquis de la Fayette, who never chanced to meet the daughter of Thomas Jefferson without pausing to exchange a few merry words with her; and of her enthusiastic admiration for Madame de Stael whom she saw very often in society, and to whose wonderful conversation she listened attentively from a respectful distance.

We are told that Patsy was allowed to go to three halls a week but never to a fourth, no matter how "tempting" that fourth might be; her father was not willing to have her sacrifice her health to the frivolities of the French capital; and we discover that upon one occasion she danced eight times with one of the Polignac family and upon another occasion was complimented on her steps by the Duke de Fronsac, afterwards to be known as Duke de Richelieu.

We learn that Patsy made the acquaintance of the celebrated Georgiana, duchess of Devonshire, and that at a certain dinner party, where she and the duchess were guests, the beautiful Georgiana smiled upon her in the height of her stature and exclaimed, "It gives me great pleasure, Miss Jefferson, to see any one as tall as myself."

At the time of Patsy's debutanteship the murmurings of the Revolution had already begun. She was in Paris when the king was brought from Versailles. The whole population of the city had turned out into the streets and such an uproar of excitement Patsy never before remembered to have heard. She and some of her young friends looked down upon the crowd from a broad window and watched the procession that was escorting the king to his captivity. As the king's coach was passing under their window Patsy and her companions recognized an acquaintance in one of the king's chamberlains, and the young chamberlain looked up and saluted the vision of fluttering handkerchiefs and smiling faces in the window above him.

The king's coach passed by and then came more cheering and renewed shouts. The noise, we are told, was like "the bellowing of a thousand bulls." It came nearer and nearer and was taken up by those around her, and Patsy at length distinguished the cry "La Fayette! La Fayette!" In a burst of enthusiasm she leaned far out of the window as a gentleman in a plain frock coat came riding carelessly by. The gentleman raised his eyes and met the eager gaze of Thomas Jefferson's "little girl" and with a friendly smile of recognition he lifted his hat to her as he passed on. Immediately Patsy's young friends crowded about her, expressing their envy of her, and Patsy herself declared that never before had she been so proud of a bow.

Upon another occasion in this period of revolutionary beginnings, just after the French officers had assumed the tricolored cockade, Patsy was at a party in one of the country residences near Paris. There were a number of French officers present and the talk even in the midst of dancing and flirtation turned upon liberty and democracy. We may imagine that Miss Patsy, who had inherited her father's broad ideas, had much to say on both these subjects. In the course of the conversation it was proposed that the officers should transfer their cockades to the ladies. The suggestion met with universal approval. So the cockades were transferred and for the remainder of the evening the French tricolor shone resplendent on the ladies' pretty ball gowns. Patsy's tricolor was treasured by her always and its history was never told until, years after, it was discovered, lying among some other precious keepsakes, by one of Patsy's own daughters.

Patsy, of course, had numerous admirers among the French officers whom she met at balls and parties. It was hinted that several efforts had been made to keep her always on the French side of the Atlantic. But Patsy loved her home and her father and sister too dearly to think of resigning them for the sake of any gallant of King Louis' court, however charming. Moreover she knew that in her own country there was waiting for her some one infinitely superior to any one whom she might meet abroad.

Along with her many happy memories of the old days at Monticello Patsy retained a very vivid recollection of Tom Randolph. He was her second cousin and her playfellow as well. He had always been a big, strong, kind-hearted chap, and, during his numerous visits to the "little mountain," had won Patsy's heart by his skill in all things and his kindness towards herself. Cousin Tom, she had discovered, could do everything from riding her father's wildest colt to pronouncing the most difficult words in her own little primer. And, what she most admired in him, he was not a tease like other boys, but was very gallant and used often to take her for a ride with him through the woods and meadows about her home or draw his chair beside her of an evening after the candles were brought in and help her with her troublesome lessons.

Patsy had not seen her Cousin Tom since the days of their pleasant girl and boy friendship in old Virginia until, a short time after she left the convent, she and her father were surprised one evening to receive a call from a tall, athletic-looking young man who introduced himself to them as Thomas Randolph. He came to them fresh from his four years of study at Edinburgh University, where he had distinguished himself as a student of the first rank and a man of brilliant promise. He was about to return to America, he said, but he could not go without stopping to see his distinguished kinsman Thomas Jefferson and his old-time playfellow Patsy.

Mr. Randolph's stay in Paris was necessarily short, but in the few weeks that they enjoyed together Miss Patsy and he learned to know and like each other better than ever before. And perhaps it was Cousin

Tom quite as much as Papa Jefferson who influenced Patsy to abandon all thoughts of a nunnery and remain in a selfish, naughty, but very happy world where she might choose as her vocation that of loving and being loved.

Cousin Tom had returned to America but Patsy still lingered in the midst of the gayeties of the French capital. She and her father and Polly, in spite of the interesting and exciting life which they led there, were longing for home, and it was with great joy that they received news of Jefferson's long-hoped-for leave of absence from Congress. Very soon after the receipt of this news, in the autumn of the year 1789, five years after that autumn which had found Patsy a lonely, homesick little girl in the Abbage Royale de Panthemont, they took an affectionate leave of their friends in Paris and set sail for America. After a fairly comfortable passage of thirty days they arrived safely and happily on the shores of their own country.

They landed in Norfolk, and the journey from Norfolk to Monticello was taken in easy stages, stopping at the houses of relatives and friends along the way, where they were warmly welcomed and hospitably entertained by those from whom they had so long been parted.

Mr. Jefferson's slaves had been notified of the family's approaching return and the day of the arrival was given to them as a holiday. They walked down the mountain to Shadwell, which was four miles distant, to meet their master and young "misses," and when at last they caught sight of the coach and four the air rang with their enthusiastic greeting. The horses were "unhitched," we are told, and the delighted crowd drew their master's carriage up the mountain to the doorway of his home.

Great was the surprise and admiration of the devoted negroes when Patsy and Polly stepped out of the coach. The girls had left little children and had returned, Patsy in the dignity of her seventeen years and high stature, and Polly in her eleventh year, more beautiful and lovable than ever before. "God bless you's" and "Look at the chilluns" were the expressions on all sides, and "Ain't our Miss Patsy tall?" and "Our dear little Polly, bless her soul." It was a home-coming such as made the hearts of the young "misses" thrill more and more with love for old Virginia.

And yet, in spite of the delight that they all experienced at being once more in their own land, among their own people, and in the midst of their own beautiful hills and meadows, there was in their home-coming a certain feeling of loss and regret. Patsy had to confess that most of the people who lived in the vicinity of the "little mountain" were stupid and "poky," and that the life which many of her neighbors led was very primitive, almost "barbarous" in its extreme simplicity and its absence of all amusement and excitement. She missed the gay scenes and the brilliant company that she had enjoyed in Paris and the change from the metropolis of the world to the quiet uneventful life about her was at first very hard.

However, it was not ordained that Patsy was to spend much time or thought in repining for lost benefits. During the months that followed her return, Mr. Thomas Mann Randolph, of Tuckahoe, was a constant visitor at Monticello and on the 23d of February, 1790, Miss Patsy and her cousin Tom were married. Patsy became a wife and in the novelty and congeniality of a happy married life she was able to forget any longings that she may have cherished for a society and existence that had passed beyond her reach.

Patsy's days were full of sweet content. She was happy in her husband, a man, so Jefferson informs us, of "science, sense, virtue, and competence," with whom she read and studied and led an "ideal family life." She was happy in her father, whom she saw honored and beloved by his countrymen, raised from one high position to another until at last he stood in the forefront of a nation. She was happy in her sister, little Polly or Maria, as she came to be called, who grew up a timid, affectionate, and very beautiful woman with regular features and "glorious" auburn hair, and who married Jacky Eppes, the favorite cousin, for whom in her childhood she had grieved so piteously when the hateful ship bore her away.

One loves to read of Patsy as a wife and daughter and sister. She was so full of pride and love and devotion for those who were dear to her. But perhaps it is as a mother more than in any other relationship that the sweet unselfishness of her character shines forth with most charm. Her home at Edgehill, the Randolph estate, from which in winter when the trees were bare, she could see the glimmer of the white columns of the portico at Monticello, was inhabited by a host of little people, twelve in all, five sons and seven daughters, of various dispositions and acquirements, but all equally interesting and lovable in their mother's eyes. There was Anne, the eldest, the fair-haired little darling, of whom in her babyhood her grandpa declared "even Socrates might ride on a stick with her without being ridiculous,"—she grew up a beautiful, much admired woman and married when she was quite young a Mr.

Blankhead; there was Jefferson, the "heavy-seeming" small boy who became "the man of judgment," the "staff" of his grandfather's old age; and there was Ellen, the bright little scholar, who developed into an intelligent and delightful woman and married Mr. Coolidge of Boston; then there were Cornelia and Virginia and Mary, all dear little girls who made very attractive and cultivated women; and there was another daughter who did not live to grow up, and James Madison, the baby of the White House, named after the revered statesman friend of all the little Randolphs and their grandpapa; there was Benjamin, the practical and energetic, and Lewis, who became a brilliant lawyer, handsome, graceful, and winning, full of life and talents, a most charming member of the home circle; and lastly there were the babies, Septima, so called because she was the seventh daughter, an unstudious, naughty, merry little child, and George, the brave sailor boy whose affection for his mother was the "passion" of his life.

With all her children Mrs. Randolph was "gentle but firm." She never spoke harshly to them, but the little Randolphs understood that when "Mamma" said a thing she meant it and that the only course for them was to do exactly as she said. Mrs. Randolph was the only instructor her daughters (with the exception of little Septima) ever had and few women of their time were better educated than the Misses Randolph. Every day she talked French with them and gave them her own broad views of history and literature. She taught all her children, both sons and daughters, to love music and recommended it to them "not so much as an accomplishment as a resource in solitude;" and perhaps the pleasantest picture we have of Patsy as a mother is that in which we see her seated at her harpsichord with her children all about her, playing and singing to them in the quiet twilight.

The most enjoyable times for Patsy and her children were the jolly vacation months when, with the coming of summer, President Jefferson retired from Washington and his affairs of state, and stopping at Edgehill, picked up the whole Randolph family and carried them all off with him to Monticello. There, on the summit of the little mountain, with its broad sweeps of vision, and the wild freedom of its breezes, was an ideal playground. The lawns and terraces about the house became the children's racecourse, and great was the fun when grandpapa arranged the young folks all in a row, giving the smallest one "a good start" by several yards, and with a "one, two, three— go!" and a dropping of the white handkerchief, sent them all off on a run, and awarded the victor with a prize of three figs. The flowers became the children's playfellows. Their grandfather taught them to love and respect the pretty blossoms, never to handle them roughly, or to disturb them in their comfortable beds. And in order to impress the children with the dignity of their floral acquaintances, he gave the flowers real names, and very amusing it was to hear the little people calling out in great glee, "Come, Grandpa! Come, Marcus Aurelius has his head out of ground." "The Queen of the Amazons is coming up."

At Monticello the out-of-door world was certainly a joyous one, and so too was the world within doors. There the enjoyments were romps in the hall, and school in the splendid billiard room. But the best indoor times came on cool evenings, in the half hour of twilight before the candles were brought in, when the children all gathered with their mother and grandfather round the fire, and engaged in such games as "Cross Questions," and "I love my love with an O." It was pleasant, too, though almost too quiet for the restless spirits later in the evening, when the candles arrived and grandfather retired to his book, and all the children followed his example and retired to their books; then often, in that hour of literary calm, grandfather would raise his eyes from his own book and look around on the little circle of readers and smile, and make some remark to mamma about her "studious sons and daughters."

It was a happy home life that was lived at Monticello. But, unfortunately, it was forever being interrupted and disturbed; there was company, more company, always company at Monticello. Hospitable as Jefferson and his daughter both were, they could not help giving way to an occasional murmur over their interminable list of visitors. Mrs. Randolph complains of being "always in a crowd, taken from every pleasing duty to be worried with a multiplicity of disagreeable ones, which the entertaining of such crowds of company subjects one to;" and Jefferson declares that he "pants for that society where all is peace and harmony, where we love and are beloved by every object we see; to have that intercourse of soft affections crushed and suppressed by the eternal presence of strangers goes very hard indeed, and the harder as we see that the candle of life is burning out, so that the pleasures we lose are lost forever."

A great interruption to the domestic "peace and harmony" of the Monticello home life, even a greater interruption than the eternal presence of visitors, was the public career of the head of the family. Jefferson's term of service to his country was a long one, and during most of it he lived away from home, alone, without the cheering society of his daughters and grandchildren. Family and household matters kept Mesdames Patsy and Polly away from their father in his public office. While he was at Philadelphia and Washington officiating first as Secretary of State, and later as President, he was obliged to call on outsiders to preside at his table and do the honors of his home. It was not until the winter of 1802-3 that the busy young housewives were able to make the long promised visit to the White House, and bring to the Presidential Mansion the genial homelike atmosphere that always hovered about Monticello.

From the obscurity of their Virginia homes the two sisters came and took by storm the capital of the nation. For the first time, since their girlhood days in Paris, and the court of Louis XVI., they became a part of the gay world. They went through the usual round of balls, parties, and dinners, and enjoyed themselves exceedingly.

In after years Mrs. Madison delighted to describe the impression made by these two daughters of President Jefferson upon the society of Washington. Mrs. Eppes, she said, captivated all by her loveliness and grace, and Mrs. Randolph by the charm of her manner and conversation drew about her, wherever she went, a circle of interested and admiring listeners.

It was very pretty, too, so we are told, to see the adoration of each sister for the other. Each earnestly wished to be like the other. Polly would sigh for Patsy's brilliancy and Patsy would retort "Oh, Maria, if only I had your beauty." Polly believed that Patsy possessed all the learning and accomplishments that could be had, while Patsy thought that her little sister was the most beautiful woman in the world.

It is certainly a delight to read of the love of these sisters for each other. But the story of their love becomes almost pathetic when we reflect upon the premature death of the one and the bitter loss of the other. During the greater part of the last days together they were alone. Their husbands, members of Congress, were at Washington with their father. Patsy had taken Polly home with her and during the days that were "a period of great physical suffering to one and of the keenest mental anguish to the other," she was Polly's nurse and mother as well as sister. Then, as time went on and Polly grew no better, Jacky Eppes came hurrying home anxious and heavy hearted, her father followed, and it was with those that she loved first and last about her that sweet little Polly Jefferson Eppes faded out of existence. Her life had been like that of a fair and delicate flower born to an early death.

The loss of their dear Polly drew Patsy and her father more closely together than ever before. They became more and more necessary to each other's happiness and their continued separation from each other seemed to them almost unbearable. It was, therefore, with more than usual delight that they welcomed the time that brought Patsy on a second visit to the Presidential mansion. She came in the winter of 1805-6, and upon this occasion she brought her whole family with her, a family which at the time consisted of one son and six daughters. Her second son, James Madison, was born during this very visit and enjoyed the distinction of being the first child born at the White House.

During this winter spent at the President's home, Mrs. Randolph was very happy entertaining her father's distinguished guests and taking part in all the gayeties of the capital. She was everywhere admired. Many were the "encomiums" bestowed upon her. The Marquis de Yrujo who was then Spanish Ambassador at Washington declared that she was fitted to grace any court in Europe and John Randolph of Roanoke was so impressed with the beauty of her mind and character that years after, when her health was proposed at a gentleman's table in Virginia, at a time when "crusty John" himself was one of her father's bitterest political foes, he seconded the toast with the exclamation "Yes, gentlemen, let us drink to the noblest woman in Virginia."

Upon the occasion of this second visit to the White House, Mrs. Randolph's eldest daughter, Anne, was deemed old enough to appear at a ball in Washington. For the first time in her life the young lady dressed herself in "grande toilette" and well escorted and well chaperoned she went to the ball. Mrs. Randolph, who was very near sighted and who had never seen her daughter except in the simple childish costumes which she wore at home, was filled with admiration when a certain tall fair-haired girl entered the ballroom. "Who is that beautiful young woman?" she inquired of Mrs. Cutts, Mrs. Madison's sister, who was seated beside her. Mrs. Cutts answered with a laugh. "Heavens! woman," she exclaimed, "don't you know your own child?"

In the spring that followed this winter of manifold pleasures and excitements, Mrs. Randolph with her young family withdrew from Washington society and returned to the quiet home at Edgehill. For the rest of her life

Mrs. Randolph was to live retired from the world, but busy with many duties and responsibilities. The mother of a large family, the mistress of a Virginia plantation, and with her husband's finances always in an embarrassed condition, she had much to occupy her time and thought. It is a charming domestic picture that which we have of Madam Patsy, she who had graced the finest and most aristocratic circles in the world, standing among her slaves like the Greek matron of old among her handmaidens, portioning out the wool that was to be spun and made into cloth.

In a life which was one of almost Homeric simplicity, Mrs. Randolph's recreations were her books sent her by her father, her harpsichord, the constant companionship of the children, and occasional visits from friends or neighbors. Calling as we understand it did not exist for Mrs. Randolph. In her day and in her remote part of the world, company did not come for a few hours in the morning or afternoon. They came to spend the day. Moreover, they did not wait to be invited. Very often the first intimation which a hostess had that she was to have friends to dinner was the sight of a carriage full of guests driving up to the door about eleven or twelve o'clock in the morning. The feminine portion of the company always brought knitting and embroidery with them, and great was the clattering of needles and tongues as the latest births, marriages, and deaths were discussed, together with the condition of crops and the most recent happenings in the political world.

It was a joyous time for Mrs. Randolph and for all at Edgelull when at last the adored father and grandfather returned to them, not as President of the United States on a hurried visit to his home and family, but as a simple country gentleman who was never again to be deprived of that domestic "peace and harmony" for which he had sighed so many years. When he came this time the removal to Monticello was permanent, and for the remainder of his life, Jefferson and his daughter and his daughter's family lived happily together on the summit of the little mountain, in the home that was so dear to them all.

Her father's death and the loss of this home—a loss that came because of the too generous hospitality that always existed there—broke Patsy's heart. The troubles that followed, her husband's death and the worries and vexations of poverty, found her resigned, almost unmoved. "There is a time in human suffering," she wrote pathetically in her note-book, "when succeeding sorrows are but like snow falling on an iceberg."

In spite of her broken heart, however, Patsy kept brave and cheerful. She even contemplated opening a school for the support of herself and family; but South Carolina and Louisiana proved her friends, and by the donation of twenty thousand dollars, saved her from the pain of ending her days in the drudgery of school-teaching.

Her children were her comforters. To them she wrote: "My life is a mere shadow as regards myself. In you alone I live and am attached to it. The useless pleasures which still strew my path with flowers—my love for plants and books—would be utterly heartless and dull, but for the happiness I derive from my affections; these make life still dear to me."

And it was in visiting among her children that Patsy's last days were passed. Many of them had married and gone far from the old home, so that she lived sometimes in Boston, sometimes in Washington, and sometimes at Edgehill. Perhaps it was at Edgehill, the home of her eldest son, Jefferson, that she was best contented. There she was nearest to Monticello. From her favorite window there, in the room that was always reserved for her, she could look up through a newly opened vista of trees and meadow land to Monticello, and in sight of the loved home live over again in memory the long season of happiness that had once been hers.

37139801R00029

Made in the USA
Middletown, DE
22 February 2019